Alphabet Tales

Tales

By Sarah K Major

Alphabet Tales

Ages 2 and up.

© 2006 Sarah K Major

© 2015 Sarah K Major - Revision

ISBN: 978-0-9829873-3-9
Printed in the United States of America

Design, storyline, illustrations: Sarah K Major

Published by Child1st Publications, LLC
800-881-0912 (phone)
888-886-1636 (fax)
www.child1st.com

Other work by this author:
SnapWords® sight words and stylized alphabet. *The Illustrated Book of Sounds & Their Spelling Patterns, Right-Brained Multiplication & Division, Right-Brained Place Value, Right-Brained Addition & Subtraction, Right-Brained Fractions, The Complete Sight Words in Sentences, The Illustrated Book of Sounds & Their Spelling Patterns,* and the *Easy-for-Me Reading Program.*

Philosophy

Use visual & kinesthetic elements

Young children learn most easily when material is presented in a way that is closely tied to movement and visual objects with which they are familiar. Incorporating purposeful movement and integrated visuals into our lessons will go a long way toward preventing learning problems. Asking children to learn the alphabet in sequence first works for some but falls short of what others need in order to learn. In this alphabet, each letter looks like a familiar object. For example, the silhouette of a flag looks like the letter F. The silhouette of mountains looks like the letter M. In addition, the object selected for the visual begins with the same letter sound. Body movement that mimics the shape of each letter completes the learning cycle.

Teach sounds rather than letter names

Young children learning to read don't need to know the names of the letters in order to learn to read. A word is made up of sounds that are put together meaningfully to form a word, not made up of collections of letter names. For instance, the letter A does not say "Ay" but rather is an individual sound that is heard at the beginning of words like "ant" or "Abigail."

Some children become hopelessly lost in the process when they are asked to learn the letter names first, then learn the name of an object that represents each letter, and THEN learn the sounds. They don't know how to manage all that information that, to them, seems unrelated and without purpose. If we simplify the process for them and let them understand that words are made of sounds, and those sounds are represented by symbols called letters, they have far less to manage. I have found that they somehow learn the letter names along the way.

Once I tutored a child who had repeated 1st grade and still could not decode. When he saw the word "and," he first said "A" (letter name), then he said "apple" (representative picture), and then he just shut down. He hated reading. We turned to the Alphabet Tales; he learned the simple sounds and accompanying hand motion for each sound, and immediately was decoding. It was significant to me that as he decoded, he unconsciously body spelled each sound. The visuals and motions not only taught him what he needed to know, they also provided the means for recall.

Make words from sounds as they are learned

The Alphabet Tales are not in ABC order because they are intended to be an accompaniment to the Easy-for-Me™ Teaching Manual, which has a specific order for learning letter sounds and sight words. In the Easy-for-Me™ Reading Curriculum our goal is to move beyond letter/sound recognition, and to get children reading immediately. Successfully reading a book will motivate children to learn more sounds and more words. Taking letters out of sequence allows us to first teach the sounds that will form words children can use.

Easy-for-Me™ takes the clutter out of teaching reading, presenting only the essentials in a way that is easily absorbed.

The Easy-for-Me™ Reading Curriculum provides parents and teachers with a powerful tool for teaching children to read, no matter the level of prior knowledge. The simple, concise lessons take children from the very first sound straight into the art of reading and writing. Each new concept taught is connected to the previous one so that no idea is unrelated. Children proceed through the learning process in a fashion that makes complete sense to them.

Students enjoying the Easy-for-Me™ program of study experience a careful balance between analyzing and decoding unknown words, and recognizing words on sight. Because of the direct link between reading and writing, spelling accuracy and reading comprehension are strengthened.

Initial lessons

1- Letter Sound for Aa, sight word A
2- Letter Sound for Tt
3- Blend A and T, sight word AT
4- Letter Sound for Ff
5- Blend F, A, and T to make "fat."
6- Letter Sound Cc
7- Blend sounds for "cat"

How to Use This Book

For pre-schoolers, just enjoy the stories together, at most emphasizing the letter sounds. There is no need for any additional teaching goal, nor any reason to push any certain learning concept with these children. Preschool children will absorb the letter shapes and sounds as you read and re-read the stories together, and will enter kindergarten with a solid foundation for learning.

For kindergarten-aged children, use the stories to introduce letters and sounds. After hearing the stories, children will recognize each letter symbol (much as we recognize faces we know when we see a photo), and will easily relate each symbol to its corresponding sound. The story line and illustrations naturally tie the symbol to the sound, bypassing the need for memorization.

As always, a great follow-up to reading the stories is artwork. The processing that children do during creative times deepens the impressions gained during "instructional time." Children hearing about Abner and the ants, for instance, might feel inspired to use crayons to draw the anthill and the ants that live inside it. Refer to the Table of Contents to locate follow-up activities for each story.

Contents

For Cookie Jo and Jaxson James

with so much love,
Grandma Sarah

The Story of A

© 2000 Sarah K Major

Amy's Ants on an Anthill, Actually

Behind Amy's house was a huge anthill where Anthony and Abigail lived with their friends. Under the ground were tunnels for food, for eggs, and for baby ants.

Far away lived a big bug named Abner. Abner was not very fast, but he was very, very strong!

8

One day, Abner went for a walk. Soon he came to a huge mountain! Abner said, "I will definitely have to climb this mountain!" Abner started to climb, but very soon he was exhausted! "Whew! I don't think I can make it to the top," Abner said. "I will have to dig a tunnel through the mountain!"

Abner was not very fast, but he was very, very strong, so in a jiffy, he was coming out the other side. But when Abner popped his head out, he saw a crowd of ants shouting at him!

"You old meanie! Our tunnels are ruined! How are we going to get our food? Now we can't take care of our eggs!" they hollered.

Abner felt terrible! He had to do something! The next thing the ants knew, here came that big, wobbly bug again!

"OH NO!" they all yelled.

But when they saw Abner bringing an apple, they cheered, "YAY, FOOD!"

As soon as Abner let go, the apple started rolling down the hill.

"OH NO!" yelled the ants again.

"Don't worry! I can fix this with my stick." Abner shoved his stick into the ground and the apple stayed put. The ants didn't even mind sharing the apple with a caterpillar! From that day on, Abner and the ants were best of friends.

The Story of T

Two Tables for Toast and Tea

Abner and the ants liked to help each other.

The ants always asked Abner when they needed help lifting something heavy.

Abner wanted help finding a new place to live, so he asked Alexander over for toast and tea.

Alexander was happy to come over. He needed to ask Abner for help, too.

When the friends sat to eat, they noticed a terrible problem. Alexander could not reach the table!

First, Abner tried piling books on Alexander's chair. But Alexander felt like a big silly sitting on books!

Then, Abner had a terrific idea! He grabbed the edges of Alexander's table, and pushed hard! With a loud cracking sound, the post popped right through the table top.

Now, Alexander's table was the perfect height! So the friends sat down again and this time, they enjoyed their toast and tea.

14

The Story of F

Fancy Flying Flags

After dinner, Abner asked Alexander what he wanted to talk about.

"There are so many anthills," explained Alexander. "If we fly a flag by our anthill it would be easier to find our way home."

"How can I help?" asked Abner.

"We need to dig a hole for the flagpole," answered Alexander.

The next morning, Abner started to work. He wasn't very fast, but he was very, very strong! Soon dirt was flying! Then Abner heard a voice behind him.

"Yoo hoo, Abner! Look here!" It was Abigail holding a flag!
"What a fabulous flag!" Abner exclaimed.

Then Abigail showed Abner another flag that was even finer than the first one.

"We can't decide which one we like better, so we want both of them!"

"I guess I need to dig another hole," Abner said.

Abner got right to work, and soon two fancy flags were flying by the anthill. Abner and the ants gathered around to celebrate.

The Story of C

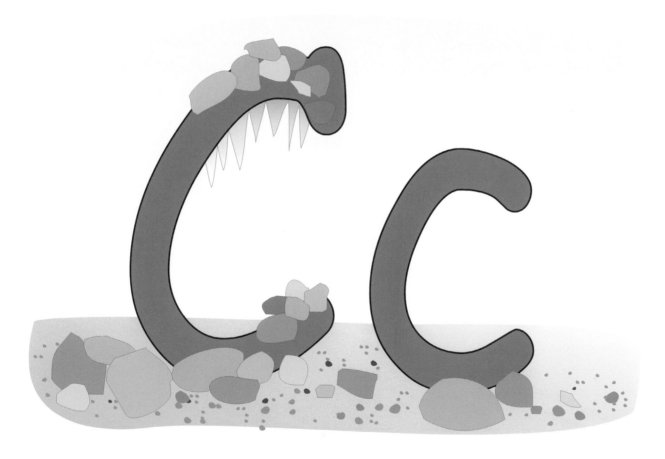

Abner Finds a Cozy Cave

Alexander suddenly remembered that Abner needed his help with something.

"Abner, how can I help you?" asked Alexander.

"I need to find a new place to live," Abner said. "Would you help me search?"

Alexander knew of a great place to show Abner, so the friends set off right away.

Soon they came to a tall tree with a large knot hole in the side. The friends inched slowly up the trunk and finally reached the hole.

Abner wheezed, "Whew, I'm tired! I'm not sure this is the right place for me!"

Next, Alexander showed Abner a dark tunnel that shot straight down into the ground. "This is perfect for you!" Alexander said.

Abner looked into the black hole. He felt dizzy. "I-I-I-I couldn't live in there," he stuttered.

That made no sense to Alexander, but he just said, "Don't worry! We'll find a good home for you."

And they did! After wandering around some more, the friends came upon two caves.

"This cave is perfect for me," Abner sighed happily.

And he moved right in.

The Story of S

Spotty Snake Slithers Side to Side

Abner was as happy as he could be in his new home. One morning, he walked outside to admire the sunrise.

"Ahhh, this is sublime!" he said, stretching his arms and looking all around. "G-good gracious! I've never noticed that stick behind my cave before! And what an odd speckled stick it is," he said, moving in for a closer look.

Abner looked way up to the top of the stick. He saw an EYE staring down at him, and a curly tongue flickering in and out of a wide mouth! "YOU'RE NOT A STICK!" yelled Abner, too surprised to be afraid. "WHAT ARE YOU?" he shouted even more loudly.

The stick-that-was-not-really-a-stick hissed, "I am a s-s-s-s-snake. My name is S-s-s-s-spotty S-s-s-s-snake. What is-s-s-s your name?"

"I'm Abner!" shouted Abner. "Why don't you come down here where I can talk to you without screaming?"

"S-s-s-s-s-so I will; s-s-s-s-so I will," hissed Spotty Snake. And he did.

First he bent this way, then he bent that way, and when he was finished bending, Spotty was low enough for Abner to talk to him without shouting.

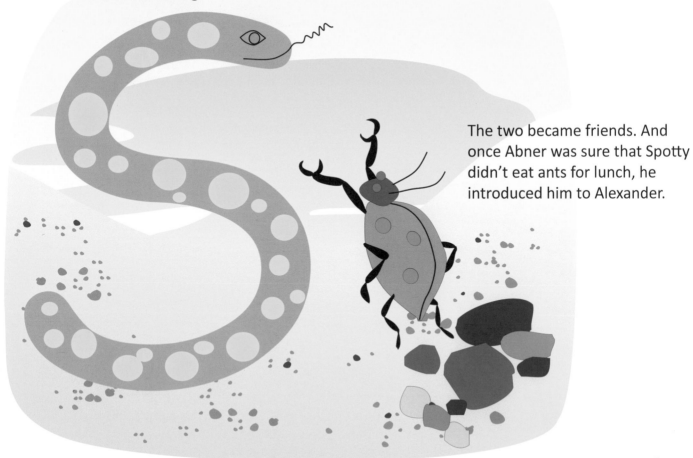

The two became friends. And once Abner was sure that Spotty didn't eat ants for lunch, he introduced him to Alexander.

26

The Story of O

Oscar Ovall Offers to Open

Remember Amy who had the huge anthill behind her shed? Well she had a little brother named Oscar Ovall.

Oscar and Amy were not anything alike, they were opposites. Amy was seven and loved to talk. Oscar, however, was five and didn't talk at all.

In fact, Oscar never made a sound! If he wanted something, he would just point to it.

Oscar's dream was to go hiking in the mountains with his older brothers. Every year, he watched his brothers go on their backpacking trip. Every year, Oscar was too young to go with them. He thought... maybe this year he could go!

Oscar prepared for the trip, just in case. He ate all his vegetables at dinner. He did 10 jumping jacks and 2 pushups. He ran around the house in his hiking boots, wearing his backpack.

All this time, Oscar Ovall never said a word. In fact, he did not open his mouth at all except to slide his spinach in.

Then the day arrived when Oscar's brothers began to pack their hiking gear. Oscar walked over to them and pointed. But his brothers said, "Oscar, you can't go. You're still too young. Why, you don't even talk yet!"

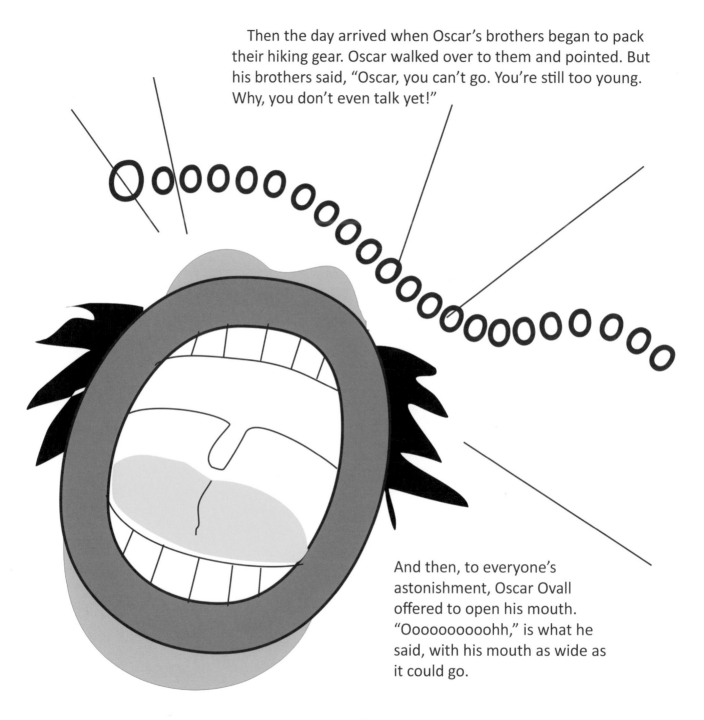

And then, to everyone's astonishment, Oscar Ovall offered to open his mouth. "Ooooooooooohh," is what he said, with his mouth as wide as it could go.

The Story of P

Pete and Paul Proudly Put on Packs

Pete and Paul were Amy and Oscar's older brothers. Pete and Paul went backpacking in the mountains every year with other hikers who also lived in Alphabury Wood.

They packed their purple packs full of things they would need for their trip: pajamas, peanuts, paperback books, and extra pants in case they got wet or muddy.

But Pete and Paul were worried. Last year, they got separated and when they couldn't find each other, they panicked. They didn't want that to happen again!

"What shall we do?" Pete asked.
Paul thought. "I know! Let's go see Mr. Luther! He'll know what to do!" So Pete and Paul picked up their packs and set off to see Mr. Luther, the mayor of Alphabury Wood.

Mr. Luther said, "Nice purple packs you have there, boys. You should also wear purple clothes so that you can find each other quickly when you are backpacking. Now... what can I do for you boys?"

Pete and Paul shouted, "NOTHING, Mr. Luther! Thank you!" Then the boys dashed home to finish packing.

Old Mr. Luther just shook his head, "I wonder what that was all about!"

The Story of M

Many Men Mountain Climb in May

Pete and Paul were finally ready for their hike.

On their first day, the hikers climbed the first mountain peak and hiked back down the other side, where they camped by a marsh.

The next day, the hikers climbed up and down a second mountain. At the bottom was a steep cliff. Every year the hikers tried to climb this cliff. No one had ever managed to do it!

Everyone wanted to make it to the very top. The climb began. Some hikers dropped out right away, but Pete and Paul munched their snacks and kept right on going! Up and up they went, higher and higher. Until...they were standing...

...right at the top! From far below, the hikers yelled, "You did it! What do you see up there?"

Pete and Paul looked around, "Well, what we see is two little round, mountains," they called.

"What they see is two little, round mountains," said the hikers to each other. When Pete and Paul had made it down again, they all went home.

The Story of D

The Dees Devour a Dozen Donuts

Mr. Dee and his son, Don, went on the hike with Pete and Paul. They liked hiking with their friends!

But by the end of the hike, their feet hurt, their backs hurt, and all they could do was moan and groan.

Don complained, "We have gone on these hikes before, and never felt like this afterwards! What is going on?"

They moaned and groaned some more, but then they figured out what was wrong.

A brand new donut shop had opened in Alphabury Wood, right on their street! Every time the Dees went outside, they smelled a delicious donut smell!

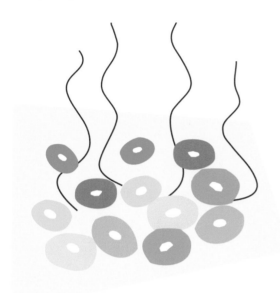

The Dees started buying a donut every Saturday morning. At first they ate just one donut.

Before long, the Dees began to get two donuts each; then three donuts.

Before they knew it, they were devouring a dozen donuts a day!

Mr. Dee and Don were getting bigger and bigger!
"No wonder my feet hurt," said Don.
"No wonder my back is killing me," said Mr. Dee.
"We must stop eating a dozen donuts a day!" they said.
"Let's just eat one donut on Saturday morning!"

The next time the Dees went on a mountain climb, they did just fine! No sore feet for them!

The Story of H

Hank and Hal have a Hanging Hall

Hank and Hal lived in two castles in a field of holly trees and flowers. A very long path curved through the field from one castle to the other.

When Hank visited Hal, he would hike down the long, winding path to Hal's castle. Hal did the same when he visited Hank.

Soon, Hank and Hal got tired of the long walk. They met one day to figure out what to do.

44

They both had some great ideas! Hank tried a pogo stick, which let him take big kangaroo hops. But Hank bounced so high he landed in the lake! Glug, glug. "No more pogo sticks for me!" he said.

Hal tried a skateboard, but he was so busy watching a spotted snake hurry across the road, that he forgot to look where he was going. SPLAT! Right into a holly tree he went! "No more skateboards for me!" said Hal.

Finally, the boys went to see Mr. Luther for help. "Build a hanging hall between your castles," Mr. Luther said.

The boys were so grateful to Mr. Luther that they built him a castle next to theirs. But Mr. Luther's hallway curved gently to the ground so he could slide down whenever he wanted to.

The Story of G

Gary Gorilla Getting Green Grapes

Spotty Snake lived in a cave by Abner. He went out one morning to search for berries to eat.

Arriving at the berry patch, he saw a small black hill lying right in front of his favorite bush. "How odd," Spotty Snake said. "This-s-s hill was not here yes-s-sterday!"

Spotty started slithering over the hill to reach the berries, but just as he got to the top, the ground shook, and he heard loud rumblings. "Goodness-s-s-s! It must be an earthquake!" poor Spotty hissed.

"I'm not an earthquake," the hill growled. "I'm a gorilla, and my name is Gary."

"But why are you sleeping here?"

"I don't have any other place to live," Gary answered.

"Come live with me," Spotty said.

Everything was fine at first. But soon, Gary started to lie around and snore. He ate fish and threw the bones on the floor. Spotty couldn't stand it anymore.

One morning, Gary heard a loud pounding noise! He went out and saw Spotty Snake, hard at work with a hammer and nails.

"Gary," Spotty said, "I made a table for you to sit at when you eat. Also, please don't throw your fish bones on the floor."

"One more thing. You are starting to take up a lot of room in the cave. Why don't you jog to the pond every time you go fishing? And how about eating some great, green grapes with your fish?"

So Gary jogged to and from the pond every day. He sat nicely at the new table, and, instead of throwing his fish bones on the floor, he put them under a bush behind the cave. Gary even began to enjoy green grapes!

The two friends lived together quite happily after that.

The Story of L

Little Larry Likes a Lavender Shoe

Next door to the Dee family lived two brothers named Lou and Larry. They looked a lot alike; in fact, people got them mixed up all the time.

There was one thing that was different about Lou and Larry, though. Whenever they went out to play, Lou walked right out and started to play. But Larry tipped over all the time.

One day was particularly lousy. It had rained hard the night before. The earthworms had come up to the top to get away from the water soaking the ground and were lying around everywhere.

Lou and Larry went outside to play but before Larry had taken two steps, over he went, face-first, right into the mud! When Lou helped him up, he saw an earthworm was stuck to Larry's front tooth!

Lou had to do something to help Larry. "I know!" Lou shouted, "Let's go see Mr. Luther. He will tell us what to do!"

The boys told Mr. Luther all about Larry's problem. Mr. Luther said, "I'm going to have to think, but I will come to see you tomorrow."

The next morning, the doorbell rang. There stood Mr. Luther holding a long box. "I've got something for you, Larry!" Mr. Luther said. When Larry opened the box, out fell the most lovely, long, lavender shoe! Quickly he put it on, and guess what? Larry never, ever tipped over again!

The Story of I

Ivan & Ichabod in a Plains Indian Camp.

After the mountain hike, the hikers always went to see Ivan and Ichabod in their Native American Camp. Ivan and Ichabod had created a Plains Indian village like ones from long ago.

Ichabod and Ivan got leather and made teepees and clothes. They made a corral for the horses, and a smoke-house. Everything looked as real as could be.

When the hikers arrived, Ichabod and Ivan talked about the Plains Indians and how they hunted for food and respected the earth.

Ichabod and Ivan decided it would be nice if their friends enjoyed a feast after their long journey.

So, they all picked berries, caught fish, gathered corn, and hunted turkeys and venison in the woods. At the end of the feast, everyone was full!

The hikers shook hands with Ichabod and Ivan, thanking them for all their work. Ivan and Ichabod, tired but happy, waved goodbye!

The Story of J

Jax and Jo Jump for Joy

Jaxson and Cookie Jo Jolly were cousins. Their friends called them Jax and Jo for short. Their shop was called The Jolly J because Jax and Jo only sold things that started with J. In front of the shop was a jackfruit tree and grapes for jam and jelly.

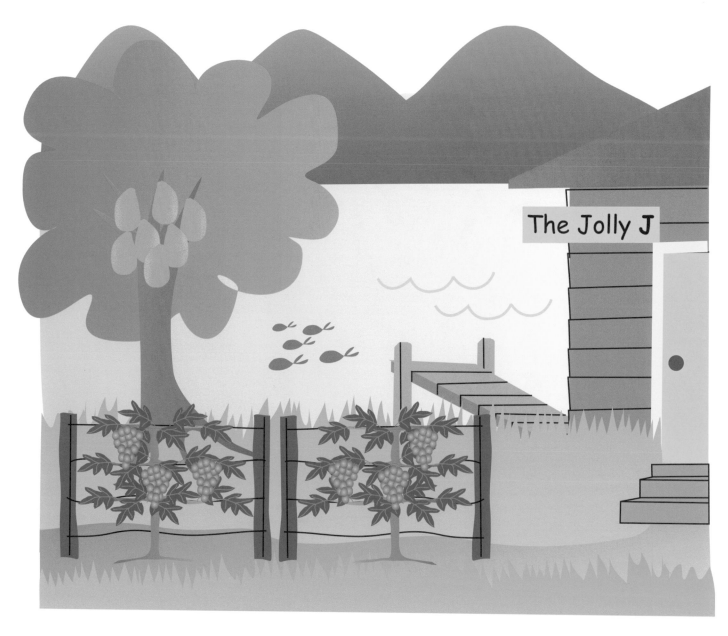

Jax and Jo made jackfruit jam and juice and also grape jam to sell in their shop.

The cousins also loved to fish. One day they were out on the lake when suddenly they felt a jerk on their line! "We've got a huge fish!" the cousins yelled.

Jax and Jo managed to get their fish into the boat. It was the biggest fish they had ever seen, and guess what?

"We caught a giant jackfish!" yelled Jax and Jo, jumping for joy.

The Story of B

Bruno and Ben Bear Become Fit

Bruno and Ben Bear were busily making umbrellas to sell in the Bear Brothers Boutique.

As they sat, day after day, all winter long, the Bears Brothers' bottoms got bigger and bigger. By spring, Bruno and Ben knew it was time to do something!

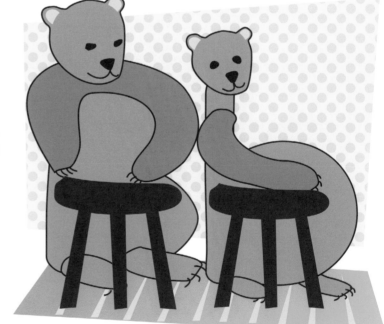

"We need to get some exercise," said the Bear Brothers. So every morning, Bruno and Ben ate a big breakfast and then set out to walk. After several weeks, the Bear Brothers were beginning to slim down.

They busily sold umbrellas to all their friends. People in Alphabury Wood used them for rainy days, and for bright and sunny days. "The sun sure is bright today!" they would say, snapping open their Bear Brothers umbrella.

The proudest day for the Bear Brothers was the day they sold a special red, silk umbrella they had spend a whole week making!

"This has been the best summer ever!" Bruno said to Ben. "We're in shape again, and best of all, Uncle Ule bought our beautiful red umbrella!"

The Story of W

Wonderful Wayne and Wanda Walrus

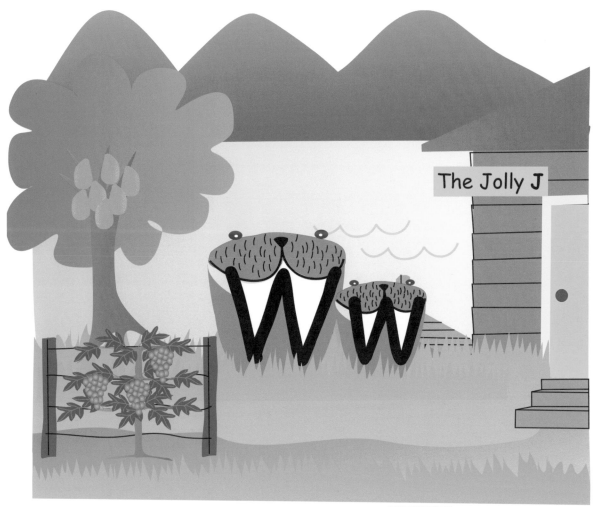

Wanda and Wayne Walrus lived in the pond behind The Jolly J. Every day Jo and Jax would throw fish high into the air and the walruses would leap up and catch them. They also swam together and wrestled at the edge of the water.

"Wayne and Wanda are wonderful walruses," Jo said to Jax.

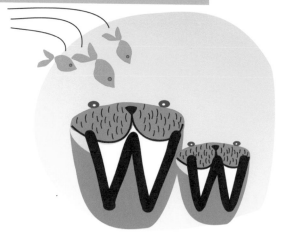

68

But this summer the walruses were not happy. Suddenly everyone was buying the Jolly's juice and jam like crazy! They also were super excited about buying jackfish. So these days, instead of playing with Wanda and Wayne, Jax and Jo worked all day.

Wanda and Wayne were worried. They didn't want Jax and Jo to work! They just wanted to play! "Let's make a plan," they said.

After the Jollys went home for dinner, Wayne and Wanda waddled over to the ice chest and gobbled up all the jackfish! But unfortunately this didn't give Jo and Jax time to play! Instead, they had to spend even more time fishing!

Wayne and Wanda realized that their plan hadn't worked! They made a new plan. They decided to help the Jollys catch fish. With all four of them fishing, the Jollys finally had time to play with Wayne and Wanda again.

"What wonderful walruses you are, Wayne and Wanda!" said Jo and Jax.

The Jolly J

The Story of R

Rebecca Roberts, Ready to Run

It was the beginning of summer and everyone in Alphabury Wood was getting ready for the Start of Summer Celebration. Rebecca Roberts was so excited! She was a runner, and she was training for the race.

Yes, Rebecca was the fastest runner ever! When she was in a race, she ran so fast that she was just a blur!

There was just one problem. Rebecca Roberts had never won a single race in her life. Can you believe that?

She'd easily pass everyone on the road, but she didn't pay attention to *where* she was going. Sometimes she ended up in a completely new town.

Rebecca was resolved to win the race. She knew she was going to have to focus on where she was going if she wanted to win.

So, Rebecca went out for a practice run, and as she ran, she reminded herself, "Watch the road! Watch the road!" This time, Rebecca didn't get lost! "I just hope I can do this well on the day of the race," Rebecca said as she walked home.

The Story of Y

Yolly and Yilly Yell, "Yippee Yay!"

Yilly and Yolly were sisters. They were very excited about the Start of Summer Celebration. Yolly and Yilly were hoping to win a blue ribbon in the cooking contest!

The rule was that you could only cook yellow things. You could not use chocolate because it's brown; you couldn't use broccoli because it is green; you couldn't use beets or radishes because they are red! No blueberries, either, because of course they are blue.

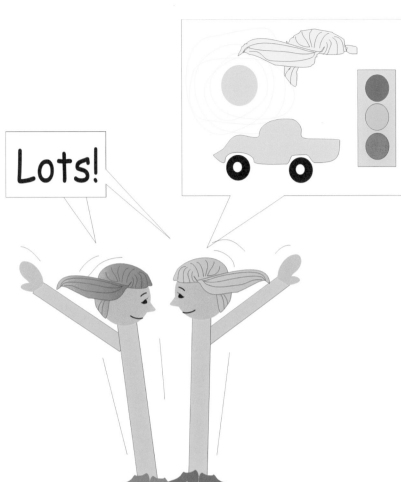

Lots!

Yolly and Yilly thought it would be fun to cook yellow stuff!

"LOTS of things are yellow!" the girls yelled in their excitement.

"The sun is yellow, your hair is yellow, Mom's car is yellow, that stoplight is yellow, the flowers in Mrs. Smiths yard are yellow, Mr. Dee's dog is yellow, Amy's shoes and dress are yellow...!" Yilly yelled.

can't

Yolly just stood there watching Yilly yell. Then Yolly said, "But we can't COOK any of that stuff, can we?" Yilly just shook her head.

Yolly said, "Bananas are yellow, lemons and summer squash are yellow, banana pudding is yellow, wax beans are yellow, pears are yellow, grapefruit is yellow. We can cook all of those."

So the girls got to work. First they cut up eight bananas. Next they poured in some banana pudding. Then the girls added a grapefruit, two pears and lots of wax beans. They stepped back to admire their work.

"Yahoo!" yelled Yolly.

"Yes!" yelled Yilly.

"Yippee Yay! We're sure to win a blue ribbon for this!" both girls yelled.

Do YOU think they won the blue ribbon?

78

The Story of N

Ned Narrow Never Notices Nelly

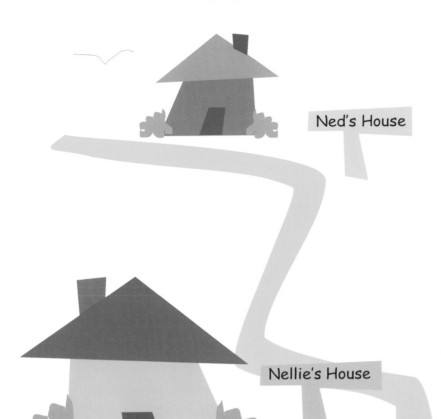

Ned Narrow and Nelly Nelson didn't see each other very often because they lived across town from each other.

Ned and Nelly were best of friends, but they were nothing alike!

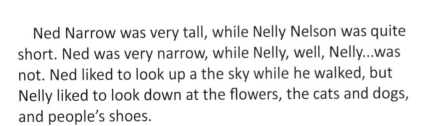

Ned Narrow was very tall, while Nelly Nelson was quite short. Ned was very narrow, while Nelly, well, Nelly...was not. Ned liked to look up a the sky while he walked, but Nelly liked to look down at the flowers, the cats and dogs, and people's shoes.

Ned and Nelly decided to go together to the Start of Summer Celebration. "Let's meet at the corner of Main and Union Streets," Nelly said.

"Sounds great!" said Ned.

On the morning of the Summer Celebration, Ned wore his best suit, while Nelly wore a new blue dress. Both set out for their meeting place.

Before long, Ned reached the corner of Main and Union Streets where he began to watch the birds and clouds.

A little later, Nelly arrived and began to admire Mr. Luther's flowers.

Then, Ned sat down to rest his long, narrow legs. He sat down right behind Nelly. Ned never noticed Nelly sitting right behind him. Nelly never noticed Ned sitting right behind her.

They sat for a very long time, waiting. Finally, when the moon came out, Ned Narrow said to himself, "I think I'd better go home."

And Nelly Nelson thought to herself, "I think I'd better go on home." So they each walked all the way back to their houses and went to bed.

The Story of U

Uncle Ule's Up-Side-Down Umbrella

Everyone in Alphabury Wood liked Ule Underwood. They called him Uncle Ule. Uncle Ule always had unusual treats and toys to share with the kids.

Uncle Ule was going to the Start of Summer Celebration to buy toys and treats. When it was time to go, Uncle Ule tucked his red Bear Brother's umbrella under his arm and set off down the road.

When Uncle Ule reached the Celebration, he went to the food tent first. There, he saw a very long table loaded down with piles of yellow food.

Uncle Ule bought brownies, pies, cakes, candy canes, and at the last minute, he bought Yilly and Yolly's Yummy Yellow Delight! Uncle Ule wasn't sure how to carry all that food home. "I know!" said Uncle Ule. "I'll use my umbrella!"

Uncle Ule opened his umbrella and then turned it upside down, pushing the point in the ground to hold it in place. And then he set all his treats inside!

"And now, for the toys!" Uncle Ule said happily to himself.

The Story of E

Eager Emmy Eats Every Easter Egg

Emmy and Oscar were friends. They were going to the Start of Summer Celebration!
Emmy couldn't wait! She loved to paint and decorate eggs. She loved to hunt for eggs. But most of all, Emmy loved eating eggs.

Emmy and Oscar hurried right over to the egg tent. Inside the tent were tables holding baskets of hard boiled eggs, paints, and brushes.

Emmy and Oscar sat down and began to paint eggs. Soon, Emmy noticed that as each child finished an egg, they ran outside and hid it in the grass.

Emmy's eyes nearly popped out of her head when she saw all the eggs in the field. "I've got to have an egg! I'll just eat one teensy one. Yummy!" she said.

When it was time for the egg hunt, the children came out of the tent. They couldn't believe their eyes. All they saw were empty egg shells!

Yes, the eggs were missing, but so was Emmy. Can you guess why Emmy was missing?

The Story of V

Volcano Valleys...Very, Very Hot!

Every year, there was a special Science Mystery Show inside a violet, velvet tent. Mr. Vine, the Science Mystery Guy, always planned the show. Soon a van pulled up next to the violet tent. The driver of the van unloaded several boxes and gave them to Mr. Vine.

Then Mr. Vine put on his velvet vest. He had jars of vinegar, some vases, and bags of clay.

Mr. Vine opened the tent flap, and everyone hurried inside! On a table were small clay mountains with deep valleys between them. At the tops of the mountains were holes.

Mr. Vine cleared his throat. "Ladies and Gentlemen," he said importantly, "Watch closely, and you will see these volcanoes erupt right before your eyes!"

Carefully, Mr. Vine poured some vinegar into the tops of the mountains. As the vinegar touched the secret ingredient inside, Mr. Vine's volcanoes erupted. Red lava came shooting out of the tops and gushed down the sides.

Mr. Vine smiled and bowed. The Science Mystery Show was over for another year.

The Story of K

Kyle and Katie Kicker, Keeping Up
Their Arms

Kyle and Katie always helped with the Start of Summer Race. "Remember how Rebecca ended up in Kokotown last year? Katie asked.

"We cannot let that happen again! We've got to help her," Kyle answered.

"But what can we do?" they asked at the same time. The twins thought for a minute and then said, "I know what we can do!" at exactly the same time.

The next morning, the twins hurried to the Celebration. They hid behind some large trees by the race track. Soon they heard the starting gun. BANG!

Within seconds, Rebecca was way out in front, but she got distracted and started into the woods! Katie jumped out from behind a tree. "GO THAT WAY!" Katie yelled loudly, kicking her foot and waving a big flag! Rebecca got back onto the path.

Every time Rebecca started off the path, Kyle or Katie jumped out and shouted. This time, Rebecca won the race!

Then the judge called the twins. "Kyle and Katie, you get a blue ribbon for kindness," she said.

Everyone in Alphabury Wood was very proud of kind Katie and Kyle Kicker.

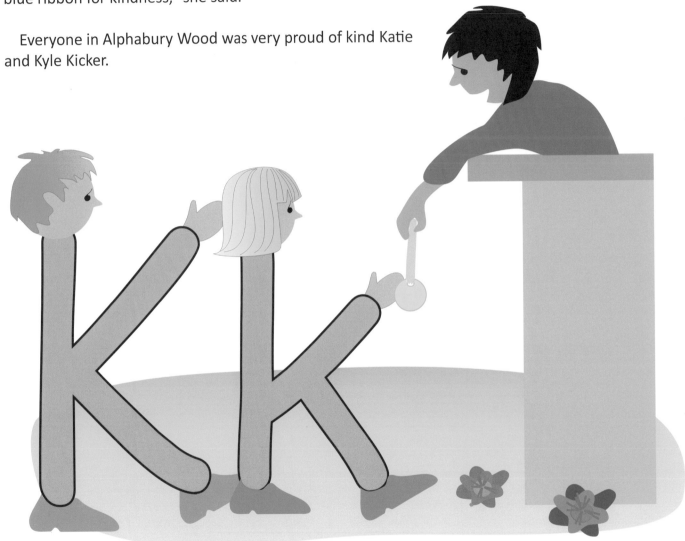

The Story of Z

Zip and Zap, Zig and Zag

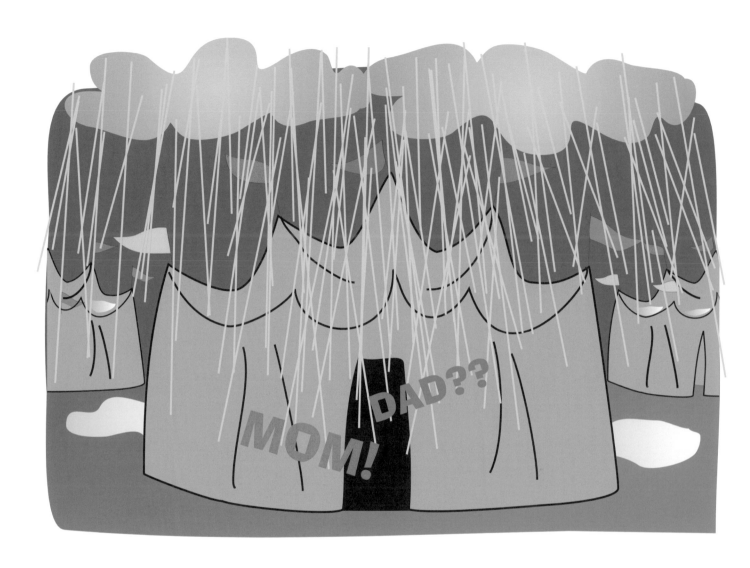

    Just as the race finished, big drops of rain began to fall. PLOP, PLOP, PLOP, PLIPPITY PLOP - faster and faster they fell. Everyone crowded into tents to get out of the rain. The sky grew so dark that no one could see anything. Thunder crashed.

    Parents called to their children, and children yelled, "MOM, DAD, where are you?" The problem was, there was so much yelling that no one could hear!

Just then, Mr. Luther grabbed a microphone and said, "Folks, may I have your attention?" Everyone stopped yelling and turned to listen to Mr. Luther. "If you will all be very quiet and patient, you will soon be able to find your lost family members," Mr. Luther said calmly.

Everyone waited quietly, just as Mr. Luther asked them to. Suddenly... there was a bright flash in the sky. The people all gasped to see Zip and Zap zigging and zagging across the sky.

Zip and Zap flashed over and over again - long enough for all the children to find their parents, and for all the parents to find their children.

"Thank you, Zip and Zap!" shouted everyone.

Then Zip and Zap flashed their brightest lights of all. "Happy to help out!"

The Story of Q

Quentin Quacks in Quinn's Quiet Pool

Quinn and his quirky duck Quentin lived by a pond next door to Uncle Ule. Quinn loved sitting by the pond, fishing, and sailing boats; in fact, anything at all that was very quiet.

Uncle Ule thought it would be good for Quinn to do things with other people. So Uncle Ule invited a bunch of kids over.

The kids sat on a quilt to eat their lunch. Quinn and Quentin were right in the middle. The kids asked Quinn lots of questions:

"Is Quentin your duck, Quinn?"

"Quack," said Quentin.

"Is that your pond, Quinn?"

"Quack," said Quentin.

"Do you fish, Quinn?"

"Quack," said Quentin.

"Can we go swimming in the pond, Quinn?"

"Quack," said Quentin.

Soon everyone was laughing. The kids were so friendly that Quinn wasn't feeling quite so shy.

Suddenly, Uncle Ule heard Quinn and Quentin yell, "LAST ONE IN IS A ROTTEN EGG!" "QUACK, QUACK." Uncle Ule was happy. Quinn's quiet pool was not so quiet anymore!

The Story of X

Xavier and Xan Do Extra Exercise

Two of Quinn's new friends were Xan and Xavier. They met at Uncle Ule's house, when Quinn learned that sometimes noise is nice.

Xavier and Xan started coming over every day to play. The three boys loved swimming, diving, and sailing boats on the pond; and they loved hanging out with Uncle Ule.

The boys' favorite thing to do was to have cannon ball contests. They would run very fast down the dock, then they'd leap into the air, wrap their arms around their legs, and make the biggest splash-landing they could.

Quack!!
Quack!!

But no matter how fast Xavier and Xan ran, no matter how high they jumped, they could never run as fast or jump as high as Quinn could. Quinn was just so... so...fast and so strong!

Xavier and Xan needed a plan. "What shall we DO?" they asked each other.

Finally they asked Uncle Ule for help. Uncle Ule leaned over and whispered. After that, every single day before Xavier and Xan went to play with Quinn, they exercised.

Before too long, Xavier noticed that when Xan ran down the dock, he was almost as fast as Quinn. And it was not long before Xan noticed that when Xavier leaped into the air, he could go almost as high as Quinn did!

ACTIVITIES FOR AFTER YOU READ

BEFORE YOU BEGIN
Before writing whole letters, practice these simple shapes and names:

1] Thin Man: | 4] Cave: C

2] Table: ———   5] Curve:)

3] Slide: \ and /   6] Hump: ∩

TIPS FOR TEACHING

1. THIN MAN: Stand up very straight and tall and have the children copy you. Say, "Start with your pencil at the top of the thin man's head and draw a line straight down to the floor!" As you say this, demonstrate on your own body, using your pointer finger as the pencil and drawing an imaginary line from head to toe. Have the children copy your motions and words. Then repeat, using paper and pencil.

2. TABLE: Draw the children's attention to a table or desk top and have them feel how flat it is. Show them that if the table is tilted, your pencil will roll off. Practice "drawing" a very flat table in the air, then repeat with pencil and paper.

3. SLIDE: Talk about sliding down a slide at the playground. You start at the top, sit down, and then slide at an angle to the ground. Mention that slides can be going in different directions. With the children, practice making your hand "sit down" at the top of a slide; then swoop and slide your hand down to the ground. Move now to pencil and paper. Practice drawing a slide down and toward you and a slide up and away from you.

4. CAVE: To make a cave with right-handed children, have them make a cave shape with their left hand, using thumb and pointer finger to make the curve. They can initially draw the cave inside this structure of their hand by putting their pencil at the tip of their pointer and then going on around until they reach the tip of their thumb. Lefties can stick their pointer finger out onto the paper, pretend it is a bear, and draw a cave around it. Practice doing this together in the air, then move to paper and pencil. See illustrations on page 6.

5. CURVE: For the curve, reverse the directions exactly from number 4, depending on if the child is right- or left-handed.

6. HUMP: Have children jump ahead a short step to simulate what they are going to draw with their pencils. Point out that they start on the ground, jump up and forward, then land back on the ground! Practice together, then move to doing it with paper and pencil.

CATEGORIES OF LETTERS

The alphabet may be grouped into categories based on how each letter is formed. What follows is one way of grouping the letters. It might be a good idea to work on the letters in one group before moving on to the next group.

Cave Letters: a, c, d, e, g, o, q, s
Children will make a cave like this:

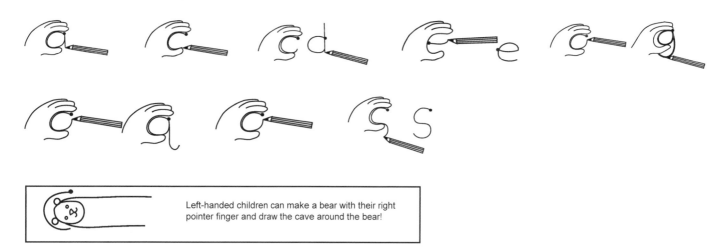

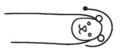 Left-handed children can make a bear with their right pointer finger and draw the cave around the bear!

Bear or Peanut Letters: p, b
The letters for "peanut butter" are made this way.

 Left-handed children can make a cave with their right hand and draw the letters inside the cave!

Slide Letters: k, M, N, v, w, x, y, z
Thin Man Letters: F, H, i, j, l, T
Hump Letters: u, (h, n, m, r)
Combo Letter: R

Aa

HAND MOTIONS:

WRITING:

Uppercase: "Start on the ground and climb to the top of the hill (make a slide going up and away from you), then sit down and slide down to the ground (make a long slide going down away from you). Next, make a table straight through the middle". Or "Climb up, slide down, then make a table through the middle."

Lowercase: "Start by making a cave, but instead of leaving the door open, make your pencil go all the way back up to the top to close the opening. Then without lifting your pencil, come straight back down to the ground (make a thin man)."

FOLLOW-UP ACTIVITY:

Give the children a sheet of paper and crayons. Let them draw large capital A's and make believe they are anthills. They can draw ants crawling up and down the sides. If you want a more involved project, let the children draw a large A and then brush glue right over the two sides with a Q-tip. They can then sprinkle sand over the glue and allow to dry before drawing their ants!

Bb

HAND MOTIONS:

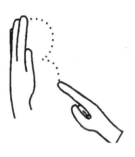 

WRITING:

Uppercase: "Make a thin man. Put your pencil back on top of his head and make a curve to touch his belly button. Next, bounce back out to make a curve that touches his toes."

Lowercase: "Make a thin man. Put your pencil on his belly button and make a curve that touches his toes."

FOLLOW-UP ACTIVITY:

Let the children make their B's and b's into bears and draw a cave nearby that they live in. Point out that their bellies both point away to the right. It is as though they are taking a walk both facing the same way. You may choose to have the children practice walking like B's do... all in a line with their bellies all going the same way. (D's do not do this, as they will soon find out!)

Cc

HAND MOTION:

WRITING:

"Put your pencil near the top line. Curve around and make a cave."

Many children have difficulty in positioning their pencil correctly when making the C. They want to start right on the top line and drop down from there. You might point out that initially what they are doing is starting just below the top line and humping up to touch the line before circling around to make the cave. See tips for making C on page 112.

FOLLOW-UP ACTIVITY:

Let the children draw bears or bats or other cave-dwelling creatures in their C's. They might even want to draw themselves camping out near the mouth of the cave.

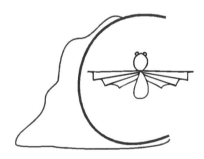

Dd

HAND MOTIONS:

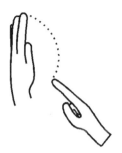 

WRITING:

Uppercase: "Make a thin man. Put your pencil back on the top of his head and make a big curve that touches his toes. He's not a thin man anymore!"

Lowercase: "Make a thin man and put the pencil on his belly button. Make a small cave that touches his toes." (Say that the D's like to talk, so their bellies are facing each other.)

FOLLOW-UP ACTIVITY:

The children can practice facing each other talking like the D's do or walking facing the same direction like the B's do. Say, "The Bb's like to walk, and the Dd's like to talk."

Let them draw shoes and hats on their D's make Dad and Don Dee.

Ee

HAND MOTIONS:

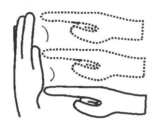 

SAY "Make your fist into an egg shape. Can you see the lowercase e?"

WRITING:

Uppercase: "Make a thin man. Put your pencil back on top of his head and make a table, pushing away from you. Put your pencil on his belly button and make a table. Then put your pencil on his foot and draw a table right on the ground."

Lowercase: "Make a table under the middle dotted line, and then without lifting your pencil, curve around to make a cave around the table."

FOLLOW-UP ACTIVITY:

Let the children decorate their capital E's to make a little girl named Emmy who wants all the Easter eggs in the playground! Their lowercase E's can be decorated with bright crayons to make Easter eggs.

Ff

HAND MOTIONS:

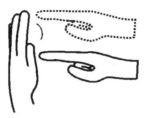 

WRITING:

Uppercase: "Make a thin man for the flag pole. Put your pencil on the top of the thin man's head. Make a table. Put your pencil on the thin man's belly button and make another table."

Lowercase: "Start on the top line, but instead of going straight down, start a curve, and then drop the line to the ground. Make a table near the dotted line that goes all the way through the thin man."

FOLLOW-UP ACTIVITY:

Children can make real flags out of a chop stick, wooden skewer, or plastic straw, adding a decorated rectangle of paper glued to the top.

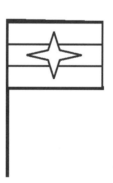

Gg

HAND MOTIONS:

WRITING:

Uppercase: "Starting near the top, make a large cave. Then make a little table to eat your lunch on."

Lowercase: "Make a little cave, and then close up the mouth.
Without lifting your pencil, drop a hook down into the basement. Make sure the hook is under the cave."

FOLLOW-UP ACTIVITY:

The child could make the upper and lowercase letters and then decorate the uppercase G as a cave with a picnic table at the entrance and the lowercase G as Gary the gorilla. Of course Gary will want some green grapes to eat on his table!

Hh

HAND MOTIONS:

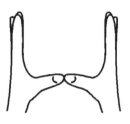 

WRITING:

Uppercase: "Make a thin man. Then make another thin man near the first. Then put your pencil on the belly button of the first thin man. Make a table that touches the belly button of the second thin man."

Lowercase: "Make a thin man. Without lifting your pencil, go back the way you came and make a hump."

FOLLOW-UP ACTIVITY:

Children can collaborate to make a capital H by standing near each other, arms against their bodies, with only their elbows bent so their fingertips touch.

They might like to draw an uppercase H and make it into a large two-story house.

Ii

HAND MOTIONS:

WRITING:

Uppercase: "Make a thin man. Put a little table on top of his head as though he's wearing a very flat hat! Put a little table under his body to make feet."

Lowercase: "Make a short thin man, and then put a dot floating above him."

FOLLOW-UP ACTIVITY:

Children can act out being capital I by standing up very straight while they say, "I am the thin man. I have a flat hat on my head (motion with their hand to make a flat table on top of their heads), and I have long, flat shoes (again, motion with their hands to signify the long, thin shoes on the floor.)"

They may draw large capital I's and decorate them as men wearing varying uniforms. They can say, "I am a fireman. I wear a red hat, and I fight fires." Or, "I am a policeman. I wear a flat, blue cap, and I keep people safe."

J j

HAND MOTIONS:

WRITING:

Uppercase: "Start at the top and go down like you are going to make a thin man. But when you get to the bottom, bounce back up a little, making a hook. Put a table on top. Make sure the hook is pointing away from the next letters so they won't get poked by the sharp point of the J!"

Lowercase: Give the same directions, but instead of making a table on top, the children will float a dot over the head of lowercase J.

FOLLOW-UP ACTIVITY:

Remind the children that sometimes when you go fishing and feel something on your line, you don't always have a fish! You might have gotten a piece of junk caught on your hook! Cut out some fish and some items that start with J and put them into an empty milk jug with the top cut off or into a plastic container suitable for this game. Have the children take turns "fishing" with their "hooks" (their little curved fingers). Enjoy seeing what each one brings up when they go fishing without looking...a fish or some J-junk!

Ideas for items: jeep, jeans, jacket, jellyfish, June bug, jerky, jet, jewels, jar of jam, jar of jelly beans, joke book, Jack-in-the-box, Jack-o'-lantern, jaguar, and so forth.

Kk

HAND MOTION:

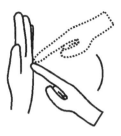

WRITING:

Uppercase: "Make a thin man. Put your pencil on the belly button and make a short slide going up and away from you. Then put the pencil back on the belly button and make a short slide going down to the ground."

Lowercase: Directions are the same except that the slide going up and away is shorter.

FOLLOW-UP ACTIVITY:

K's are fun to make with your whole body. Stand nice and tall, and then hold one arm forward at a slant, while holding your right leg out in front of you just as far as your arm is. You can have the children talk about how their leg looks like they are kicking a ball, while their arm looks like they're holding on to a kite string. They might want to draw this picture using a K as a body that is kicking a ball and holding a kite.

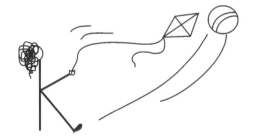

Ll

HAND MOTIONS:

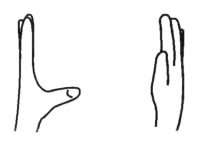

WRITING:

Uppercase: "Make a thin man, starting at the top line. Without lifting your pencil, turn right, or away from you, making a table right on the bottom line."

Lowercase: The lowercase L is just a tall thin man!

FOLLOW-UP ACTIVITY:

Children could make a child with a long, lavender shoe out of capital L and draw his barefoot friend out of lowercase L. Ask the children to make up names for their L people, ones that start with the LLL sound.

Mm

HAND MOTIONS:

WRITING:

Uppercase: "Starting on the ground, climb up the side of the mountain. When you are at the top, sit down, and slide down the other side. Climb up the next mountain, sit down, slide down, and you're done!"

Lowercase: "Make a thin man, and then go back the way you came. Make a hump. Then make another hump."

FOLLOW-UP ACTIVITY:

Have the children act out being lowercase M. First they will make a thin man by standing up very straight. Then they will take two forward hops to make the two humps of the mountain!

Have them draw M and pretend it is mountains (works best if they draw the M's nice and large). Have them put trees on the sides of the mountains, a river in the valley, and then draw themselves climbing the mountain. They could draw some animals they might find on the mountains, and a moon.

Nn

HAND MOTIONS:

WRITING:

Uppercase: "Make a thin man. Then put your pencil back on the top of the thin man's head and draw a slide moving away from you. Then make your pencil go straight back up until it touches the top line."

Lowercase: "Make a shorter thin man, and then go back up the way you came, making a hump right by the thin man."

FOLLOW-UP ACTIVITY:

Have the children draw capital N and turn him into a man sitting on the ground which we will name Ned. Ned is a narrow (thin) man who loves to eat noodles. Make lowercase N and turn it into a woman named Nelly. Ned never notices Nelly who is sitting right behind him.

If you are really brave, boil some spaghetti noodles and bring them to school. When it is time to use them, run hot water over them from the tap to soften them up again, and then let the children form Ned and Nelly out of pieces of noodles.

Oo

HAND MOTION:

WRITING:

"Make a cave, but then close up the mouth of the cave."

FOLLOW-UP ACTIVITY:

Have the children say the AH sound that is short vowel O, like the sound found in "pot." Then point out that the shape of their mouth when they say AH looks like an O! Trace around your lips with your right pointer finger while you say "ah."

Children can draw the open mouth that is the O and then make their own picture out of it. They can fill the mouth with their favorite foods that start with the short O sound, or they can make up reasons for why the owner of that mouth might be wailing!

Pp

HAND MOTION:

WRITING:

Uppercase: "Make a thin man. Then put your pencil on his head and make a curve that touches his back right at his waist."

Lowercase: Lowercase P is the same, but his thin man starts on the dotted middle line, and his legs go into the basement.

FOLLOW-UP ACTIVITY:

Let the children pretend to be P's by putting packs on their backs and pretending to go hiking in the mountains. Or they could draw themselves with their packs on, filled with all the things they would put inside. They could cut pictures out of old magazines to glue inside their backpacks.

Qq

HAND MOTIONS:

WRITING:

Uppercase: "Make a large cave, and then close up the mouth. Then put your pencil in the middle of the O and make a slide. This is the diving board for the quiet pool!"

Lowercase: "Make a little cave and close up the mouth. Without picking up your pencil, drop a thin man into the basement."

FOLLOW-UP ACTIVITY:

Children may draw large uppercase Q's and then draw their friends or family and themselves at a pool party!

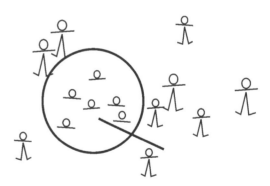

Rr

HAND MOTIONS:

WRITING:

Uppercase: "Make a thin man. Start back up with your pencil on the top of his head and make a curve that stops at his belly button. Without lifting the pencil, make a slide away from you, down to the ground."

Lowercase: "Make a short thin man. Go back up the way you came and start to make a hump, but then stop near the top."

FOLLOW-UP ACTIVITY:

Children can pose like Rebecca did (see *Alphabet Tales*) when preparing for her race: one foot out in front, their bodies leaning over, and both hands on their forward knee.

After they have practiced the whole-body R, they could draw an uppercase R and embellish it to look like a runner at the starting line.

Ss

HAND MOTION:

WRITING:

"You start to make a cave, but then as you get near the dotted line, you change your mind and decide to make a curve under the cave, facing the other way.

To make the S easier to form, have the children make a cave with the thumb and pointer finger of their right hands. The S fits nicely in and around this shape:

FOLLOW-UP ACTIVITY:

Have children make large S's and decorate them as snakes with bright markings on them.

Tt

HAND MOTIONS:

WRITING:

Uppercase: "Make a thin man by putting your pencil on the top line (top of the thin man's head) and dropping a line straight down. Start to one side and make a nice flat table on top."

Lowercase: "Make a thin man, and then make his table across his shoulders."

FOLLOW-UP ACTIVITY:

Let the children "set their tables" with their favorite food for a snack. They may draw the foods or cut pictures out of old magazines and glue them in place.

Uu

HAND MOTION:

WRITING:

Uppercase: "Starting at the top, go down, curving at the bottom; bounce off the bottom and go back to stop at the top line again."

Lowercase: "Start on the middle line and make another bowl shape. This time, when you are back up on the dotted line, draw a thin man going straight down."

FOLLOW-UP ACTIVITY:

When the children have practiced making U's, let them make Uncle Ule's umbrella by adding little curves at the top to join the two sides and drawing a curving umbrella handle. Let them decorate, if desired, and color.

Vv

HAND MOTION:

WRITING:

"Starting at the top, make a long slide moving away from you. When you get to the bottom, make a long slide going back up." Later you can say, "Slide down, and then climb back up."

FOLLOW-UP ACTIVITY:

Show the children that they can make really big V's with their arms by touching elbows in front of their bodies and making their arms slant outward. They will no doubt like to make these "volcano funnels" and make swooshing, erupting lava noises too!

Let the children decorate their V's by coloring red lava inside and curling black smoke and ash coming out the top.

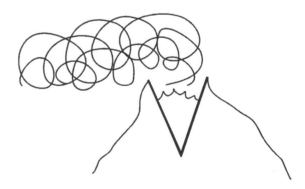

Ww

HAND MOTION:

WRITING:

"Start at the top line and make a slide away from you, down to the ground. Without lifting your pencil, climb up and away from you until you touch the top line. Make a slide away and down, then climb up and away until you touch the top line."

(Later you can say, "Down the slide, up the slide, down the slide, then up and stop.")

FOLLOW-UP ACTIVITY:

The children can make their W's into Wayne and Wanda Walrus by drawing a curve around the W's, an oval above them and adding round eyeballs at the top.

Fish are easily made by drawing curves in opposite directions and letting them intersect for a tail.

Curve   Pencil on nose, curve away.   Pencil on tip, curve to other tip

Xx

HAND MOTION:

WRITING:

Uppercase: "Start at the top and make a long slide away from you until you reach the bottom. Then put your pencil at the top again and make another long slide coming back the other way. Be sure and cross over the first slide right in the middle, on the dotted line."

Lowercase: Repeat the directions, but use the dotted line for the top.

FOLLOW-UP ACTIVITY:

Have the children make a connection between the center of the X and their waists to reinforce that the slides have to cross in the middle. Have them put their hands on the sides of their own waists to remind them of this while you talk about how to form the letter.

Have the children practice doing jumping jacks so their whole body looks like a big X. Then let them draw their X's in pretty colors and decorate them to look like kids exercising.

Yy

HAND MOTION:

Use right hand so thumb will represent the short slide in the Y.

WRITING:

"Starting in the air touching your top line, make a short slide going away from you that stops on your dotted center line. Then go back to the top line, start at the other side and make a long slide all the way down to the very bottom line. Be sure and touch the bottom edge of the short slide as you go past it."

Children can say "Little slide away from me," then "Big slide toward me."

FOLLOW-UP ACTIVITY:

Let kids draw large Y's on their papers and then make them into girls or boys who are jumping in the air with their arms out yelling "Yippee yay!"

Zz

HAND MOTION:

LH makes a slide:

RH table starts at top
and quickly moves to bottom:

WRITING:

"On the top line, make a table pushing the pencil away from you. Then without lifting your pencil, make a long slide coming toward you. Without lifting your pencil, draw a table going away from you on the bottom line."

The children might enjoy saying, "Zig, Zag, Zig" while they make each motion. Zig is the sound for the table, while Zag is the sound for the slide.

FOLLOW-UP ACTIVITY:

Let the children draw their idea of a storm and make the lightning in the sky. It would be especially effective to do this project on black construction paper and use white and yellow crayons for the lightning flashes!

Sarah K. Major is the Founder and CEO of Child1st Publications LLC. Her absolute belief in every child's ability to learn, and her passion to empower the child by supporting his/her own unique giftedness have fueled her life's work and provided a new pathway for children to succeed academically. She was the recipient of The Outstanding Parent Satisfaction and The Major Academic Program Improvement awards during her tenure as Title 1 program designer/director. Her numerous books and multisensory learning resources such as: SnapWords®, Easy-for-Me™ Reading, the Right-Brained Math Series, The Illustrated Book of Sounds & Their Spelling Patterns and more have earned a host of five star reviews, and have helped to advance the education of children around the world. Ms. Major taught preschool through the 12th grade, and holds a Master's degree in Education, and a Bachelor of Arts.

Child1st multisensory learning resources for math and reading are designed specifically for right-brained learners, including beginners, visual and kinesthetic learners, and those children who have already been labeled with dyslexia, autism, Asperger's, auditory processing disorder, ADHD and more.

For more information please visit www.child1st.com.